Vintage Visual Merchandising

The 1970's: Me & The Mannequins

Volume One 1978

By

JD Vincent

Table of Contents

FORWARD: The Mannequins

The mannequins in this book, from Bonwit Teller Chicago, came from only a few companies of the many that were around in 1978. I had a few mannequins that were there in 1977, when I first went to work at Bonwit's, and I purchased others later the following year.

I don't pretend to be a mannequin expert, but mannequins are essentially a merchandise selling tool; but, what a tool. They have been around for decades. They have evolved from being a tailor or a seamstress form model to make clothing with, to having arms, legs and a head. They can seem to be almost lifelike with hair, makeup and whatever fashion they are wearing at any given time. The best ones have almost, at times, a dreamy quality of being this fantasy creature with a soul. They are works of art unto themselves even before we put garments on them.

Some of the best of them have been sculpted out of clay first by fine artists to make the initial mold from then which many hundreds are then reproduced.

By the late 60's and early 70's (though this also occurred in the 30's – 50's as well) mannequins started to be posed in a more active ways than just simply standing. Some were modeled after real people – models, actresses etc. There was a Twiggy mannequin, a Cher mannequin – both made by the Adel Rootstein company out of the UK. Most mannequin companies had names for their mannequins and most manufactured them in a "series" that would have a name as well. Rootstein in the 70's had the "Walk & Talk" series for instance – these girls looked literally as if they were walking and talking to each other.

Most of the mannequins today – and the last few decades – are these creatures with no heads, or at best, have an alien type "egg" head making them look oddly asexual and creepy. They generally stand lifeless next to a sign. A few of the high end stores still present fashion with the "old school" mannequins – Nieman Marcus, some Macy's and New York stores like Bergdorf Goodman, Saks Fifth Ave. etc. In 1978 it was still the "norm" to have these lifelike models with hair and makeup and an interesting pose.

In my display window designs here, the design of the windows did not start with the mannequins, but as you'll find out – as I had only a few to choose from – they at times impacted the creative process.

PREFACE: "Display" vs "Visual Merchandising"

The year, in which all of this book's photographs were taken, 1978, represent one year in my visual merchandising/display career. At the time there was a professional photographer roaming the city who offered up photographs of display windows at many stores. Early on when I was Display Manager at Bonwit teller, he showed up one day with the first of some very nice photos. For $10.00 each he would continue to photograph more. $10.00 in 1978 wasn't an insignificant sum as we changed the windows every two weeks, nor was it out of my reach either.

1978 was also the only year I worked at Bonwit Teller. In late 1977 I was in between jobs. I was offered this job on a temporary basis until the current Display Manager recovered from an operation. When he decided to not return, I was offered the position permanently.

The term Visual Merchandising was still somewhat in its early days and not yet widely used — there was still some thought as to what it referred to. Merchandising racks of clothing? Merchandising shelves of product? It was kind of a loose assignation. The term really had been coined to help elevate the Display Department person to an executive level — to bring that person and department more respect and credit for the sale of the department store's goods. At Bonwit Teller at this time, it was still the Display Department.

The photographer's name eludes me now. I have no idea whatever happened to him. Every time my assistant and I changed the display windows we each purchased photographs. My assistant and I worked closely together on this — we were a team. Without her I could not have accomplished everything in this book — she complemented me at every level of the creative process. The idea or inspiration might have been mine, but she helped me to "make it work."

This year would become one of the most creative periods of my career. I was 25 years old and had already worked for three stores and been a manager for two and a half of those years. I had been creative at my previous jobs — but nothing like what this experience would become.

The following plates are some of the display windows that I created that year — though not all. I've lost many photos over the years. Not all were taken by the professional photographer, as you'll be able to see at first glance. The professional was able to eliminate most of the reflections in the plate glass — mainly by photographing in the evening. Likewise, not all of the displays were successful. But these mannequins are almost always compelling to observe.

Preceding each plate — or group of plates — is a brief description of how the display window evolved — in so much as I can remember. These are random thoughts meant to be conversational in a tone that is sort of half remembering and half guessing as to how the final results came to be. They are not, nor are they meant to be, great prose.

Plates 1, 2....A Shortage of Props

This was one of my first display windows at Bonwit's. I had not been there long enough to purchase any new props – or mannequins. The mannequins that were there, for the most part, were from DG William's. I don't recall what series they were from but almost each one of them was posed in a specific manner with their arms and/or their legs as well. They leaned, they had their arms up in the air, etc.

I thought – "What am I going to do with these mannequins who perpetually have their arms up in the air, or leaning against something?"

The Display Department had a very small work and storage area located on a hidden mezzanine level. I say hidden in that there was only one elevator – out of several - that went to the mezzanine. The mezzanine was always over-crowded with just about anything imaginable – old props, mannequins, supplies, two desks, merchandise – you name it. I was rummaging around in it one day and found this beautiful slubby, nubby raw silk fabric that was almost of a wall covering weight – like a grass cloth. It draped and formed in a very interesting manner as it was unrolled. I said to my assistant "Let's put these rolls of fabric in these mannequin arms that are up in the air" – or something to that effect.

What resulted was a deceivingly simple window display. The reaction to the window was pretty good as I recall now – it's certainly always been a favorite of mine.

Plate 1

Plate 2

Plates 3, 4, 5….Bill Blass Men's Trunk Show Window

One of my first window designs at Bonwit Teller was a Bill Blass men's window. We hardly ever used the main fashion window for men's – in fact, this is the only time I can remember doing so. These mannequins we used here were considered semi abstract in that they weren't flesh tone and had sculpted wigs.

Blass, known for his women's fashion, was also a very accomplished tailored men's wear designer. There was to be a trunk show of his Spring 1978 collection. Mr. Blass himself was to be in attendance rather than a representative. This was a pretty big deal. I was very much looking forward to meeting him. This was also January in Chicago. A snowstorm – either here or in New York - prevented Mr. Blass from attending the trunk show.

I had, however, wanted to impress Mr. Blass with my design skills – and – this was also one of my first window designs for Bonwit's. I didn't have much of a budget – and there was also short notice. I had not yet been fully integrated into the monthly store planning meetings with upper management. I really don't remember how I got approval for window designs. I never sketched them – there wasn't time.

Repetition - combined with minimalism – was my style at the time – whether it was generally in style, I don't remember. I incorporated both styles into my window designs in the 70's. There wasn't much time to gather props so I relied on my skills with foam board and fabric to create a graphically inspired backdrop for the mannequins in the Blass suits. I liked then, and still do, this type of clean, graphically inspired display window.

These are some of the photos that I had been taking myself in 35 MM slide format before the photographer found me. But, after having these slides converted after all these years, it's interesting to see in the glass reflection all of these big 70's cars – and – all of the snow. Note also that the parquet wood floor – I later installed floor pads made out of foam board covered in white vinyl.

Plate 3

Plate 4

Plate 5

Plate 6....A Swim Suit Window

By this time – May 1978 – I had more or less decided to give up on making these "Arms Up In The Air" mannequins make any sense in the context of a window display.

Department stores hardly ever in those days – or now – have any windows (real) to the outside. I've mentioned previously the exposed, structural and design element of the Hancock building's cross beams. They were noticeable inside the store everywhere except floors two and three. Walls had been put in front of them to house fixtures for merchandise. This created storage areas around the perimeter of the store on these two floors.

I found a door one day behind these walls on one of these floors and went snooping about and found basically a bunch of old fixtures collecting dust. Then, I found these very large "wedge" shaped structures in various sizes – 4 feet to 6 feet – wood framed and covered in sized canvas painted white. Maybe they had been a prop before? If not, they would be now. They were kind of dirty so I gave them a fresh coat of white paint. I decided to keep the window design very graphic and have no reference to summer or the beach. I simply painted the window walls a true "hot" orange and with the floor pads I had already covered in white vinyl, it made for a very graphic, minimal window display. A composition of just color and shapes for the mannequins in swimsuits.

This was also one of the instances where I did not utilize the whole window space and just centered the props and mannequins and left the two end areas blank except for the continuation of the orange wall and white floor to either end. Note the two mannequins in prone positions – the one to the right was modeled to be lying down. The one to the left is actually meant to be standing, but leaning against a wall. I placed her left foot to one of the wedge shapes as if she was holding it upright. I also experimented with mannequins being "unstruck" – without wires. I may have used one wire on one of them. I can't really tell from this image. At the time we also would paint the wires white if against a white backdrop – that may have happened here as well.

Plate 6

Plates 7, 8….Missoni

Bonwit's had several, "Shop-In-Shop" spaces – a dedicated area that was for that labels' use exclusively. In early 1978 the Italian fashion house, Missoni, would be moving into the front, north corner of the store with open windows. This corner of the store had the beginning of one of the iconic, structural cross beams of the building. They would first get the fashion window on Delaware, to announce their opening at the store.

In the beginning of the year, I always felt that I had to have this mannequin with the "arms up" position actually interacting with a prop – in this case holding up the "string" of one of the "hang tags". Later in the year I just gave up trying to figure out how to integrate this mannequin into something that made any sense. I suppose – as her pose suggests, I said to myself while first shrugging my shoulders: "Why bother? I'm running out of ideas".

I don't remember where we got these enlarged labels – they were probably sent from the New York office. As well, I don't recall there being any direction as to what to do with them. I thought, I suppose: "They're oversized hang tags" So I bought some rope, cut a hole at the top and attached it to the tags and let the mannequins interact with them a bit. They were simply centered in the window for a very stark, graphic display - plus – it would give that mannequin with her arms up in the air something to do.

You can see here in these two photos that they were shot by me - notice the reflections in the plate glass again – the huge 1970's cars. The snow appears to be melting a bit – so it's probably around late January or early February.

Plate 7

Another view of the Missoni
display window.

Plate 8

Plate 9…. A Men's Spring Window, White On White

Both the women's and men's display windows had parquet flooring – which was nice and very much of the era, but I always preferred the floors to match the walls – more of a blank canvas – a blank box. There's not the more obvious "break" in the horizon line - mannequins, as well as props, seem to pop out more. It appears to be more of a design composition – more painterly like.

This men's window shows this more than the woman's window because of its size I guess – it was much smaller at about 10 feet wide. I didn't like the doors of either of the windows of course – but here it is much more evident. I don't like the extra lines, it mucks up the background. What I could I do though? We had to get in and out.

The method I chose to produce the floor pads was based on my previous work at another store when I began to be influenced by New York window displays – in particular, as it worked out – Bonwit Teller. Bonwit's in New York had display windows with huge heights – at least 12 feet - the height was emphasized even more by "padding out" the entire back walls with two foot wide white, vinyl covered pads.

Floor boards were a bit more of an upkeep issue, what with all of the nail holes from striking the mannequins. They needed to be replaced often – you could only put a mannequins' foot over a nail hole so often.

Here - also more evident than previous photos – the 20 gauge mannequin wire. I painted it white, as well as the nail head itself, so it would appear to disappear. I've always liked white on white as a design theme - white merchandise, mannequin, props, floor and walls – very simple and graphic. Notice to the extreme right lower corner – the bottom corner of what appears to be a drape. This window had velvet drapes for some reason – which I hadn't remembered until now.

Plates 10, 11… The Entire 30 Foot Width – A Spring Window

I had conflicted feelings about this HUGE display window – the main fashion display window on Delaware. At times – especially early on – I wanted to utilize its extra-long width – at times I felt I had to, as in the Bill Blass window. But I was very much into minimalism at this time in my career – so it was a challenge. Other times, I would just simply ignore the outer two window glass sections (separated by the mullions) and simply center the window display.

This picture is also one of the early windows that I photographed in 35 MM slide format. Again, if you look closely you can see reflections of cars etc. Also, you can see that I was not able to capture the entire span of the three sections – 30 feet - of the window. Neither of these two shots comprises the entire display design.

I purchased this Chinese style paper kite early in 1978, not only specifically for the length of it, but, as well, that it gave these mannequins, ever with their hands and arms up in the air, something to interact with – rather than just being there up in the air with nothing to do.

Note the mannequin at the far left at the end of the kite. She had playfully kicked off her shoes, it could be assumed, in playing with the kite. Though how many women in heels play with kites, I'm not sure of – but this, after all, is the dual fantasy world of designer clothing and mannequins. Actually, my assistant usually didn't like much of the shoe selection at Bonwit's, as well as, sometimes the mannequins were hard to "strike" properly in some heels. The heel height at times did not align with the arch of the mannequins' foot. In the fast changing world of women's fashion, sometimes the mannequin manufacturers did not keep pace with the height of high heels.

The absence of shoes on a mannequin(s), or the mannequin simply holding her shoes – or – as in this case, where the heels are casually tossed aside, would be a recurring element at times in these display windows.

Plate 10

Another view of the Spring
display window.

Plate 11

Plate 12….A Barefoot Bridal Window

What would a specialty or department store window display calendar be without a Bridal window? This was probably early June.

I was never a fan of overly sentimental bridal windows – lots of flowers and cupids and what not. I wanted to try something different – plus I was still somewhat short on props. I found these ladder props somewhere in the store, painted them white – I was still at times trying to figure out a propping to give one of these mannequins something to "prop up" with their hands/arms - in this case a cloud.

Clouds – I'm not sure where that idea came from. The ladders needed to go somewhere - an atmospheric and dreamy wedding? Maybe I'm stretching a bit too much in hindsight.

I had made clouds with netting – or tulle – before, though we had used a different method in forming them. Here – and I would use this method several more times in succeeding years – I just unrolled it off of the bolt and started to form the clouds by bunching it up loosely then after I had a cloud form I wanted, tucked part of it into the metal grid in the ceiling to secure it.

Bonwit's had excellent theatrical style lighting, and I used it to full effect for every window – here to brightly highlight the "clouds". The lighting fixtures were non-traditional for display in that they were not part of a ceiling or side wall track. Each one clamped onto a pole system that, not only ran the entire width of the display window, but also ran ceiling to floor at the three mullions. Each had its' own cord – I'm not sure how many outlets were there – must have been a lot. It didn't bother me to see all of the light heads and the cords and poles. I thought that leant a theatrical flair to each window display.

The bridal gowns were stunning. Here notice we gave up any pretense on having the mannequins hold their shoes or to have them casually strewn about – we just left them barefoot. A couple of the gowns were long enough to hide this – the others not. I did take some heat on this – but management liked the display window in general, so somehow I got away with it.

The mannequins were also a bit trickier to strike without shoes – they tended to slide & fall back. Mannequin evolution had evolved at this point in time to provide a separation between the mannequins' big toe and the second – for sandals. I put a nail at that separation point/joint to secure them. If you look closely at the girl to the far right – we didn't paint the wires white – I'm not sure why.

Plate 12

Plate 13….A Men's Summer Window

Men's yellow trousers? It was the 70's. As of this writing in 2014 – color has returned to men's fashion in a big way. Not into mine, however. They say if you can remember wearing it the last time it was fashionable, you're probably too old for it this go-around.

Every so often I liked to utilize the stores' sizable cache of antiques – here a desk and chair. If I could, I liked to at least somewhat obscure the doors of enclosed windows. Here I simply propped the fantastic framed art print right on the desk and leaned it against the door and wall. I can't really tell from the picture – and don't remember – but probably the only way I got in and out would be to partially lean the print against the wall. That way, as I exited the window, I could slightly angle the print so I could squeeze past it then straighten it out again before I closed the door. Or – more likely as I was 25 at the time– I probably just crawled out under the desk and closed the door behind me.

Plate 13

Plates 14, 15, 16….The Radiator Window

By the summer of 1978, I was building up a small inventory of new props. In June I went to NADI (National Association of Display Industries) summer market in New York and purchased some new props. Here – radiators – not real but crafted out of Styrofoam from the famous Niedermaier prop house – actually located in Chicago.

Niedermier at the time, and for many years after, was the premier – the Cadillac – of display prop houses. As Rootstein was to mannequins, so Niedermaier was to props.

Stylistically, I was still moving within this minimalistic period – for the most part. Utilizing the full thirty foot width, this display window design epitomizes that look. It was with this design that the chair rail was added to the Delaware St. fashion window as a more or less permanent feature. With the simple repetition of the same prop – indeed such a mundane and unsexy prop as a radiator - and the added horizontalness of the chair rail, the elegant, sexy "little black dresses" stood out prominently.

At the time I was also experimenting with alternative mannequin placement – meaning, not just standing them there faces forward. By placing one mannequin with her back slightly turned away at the front of the window, it added interest I believed. It might make you stop and try to get a better glimpse of the front of the dress, which the photographer captured very well in the close up shot - Plate 16. He did not take that shot from inside the window as it might appear to be. It's a very sexy dress – its sexiness not immediately evident unless you stop and look.

The other close up - Plate 15 – shows again these incredible dresses - I wish I could remember the designer names. I'm not quite sure how a woman could wear the one on the right without, well, spilling out of it. Their hair styles are awfully out of date today – but were popular at the time. Think of Barbra Streisand's hair style in "A Star Is Born", released late in 1976.

Plate 14

Plate 15

Plate 16

Plates 17, 18, 19….The Store Entrance Windows

There were two revolving door entrances. This is the north entrance facing Michigan Avenue – albeit way back from the street. This is the only picture that I have that contains any of the exterior signage (Plate 17).

An open back display window was never – still isn't – the optimal way to go, I thought. I think most visual display designers would agree – as it just doesn't lend itself to a "pure" design. By that I mean, as I've stated earlier, a blank canvas – or a box to begin the design with no distraction from the store interior is the best way to go if you can. These views of the store interior are competing design elements – as here with the interior of the store visible through the paned glass wall. As beautiful as the store was, it prevented me ever doing a whole lot with these windows. I would never have, say, tried to block these paned glass back walls. For one, I don't think store management would have allowed it. I wouldn't have tried anyway; it would have just looked too schlocky.

This entrance (Plate 18) looked into the accessories department of the store – jewelry, handbags, hosiery etc. The window on the right side (Plate 19) has the interior curved wall that's covered in this beautiful gilt wallpaper. While not my style, I certainly, even in 1978 thought it was gorgeous – and likely very expensive keeping in line with the design of the store interior with its generous use of antiques in a modern setting. These two Art Deco style goat figures on the acrylic pedestals, though not part of the store's antique collection – they certainly were in that spirit.

Plate 17

Plate 18

Plate 19

Plate 20….Situation Style Lingerie Window

Not all window display designs are "For the Ages" – as in this "situation" style lingerie window display – even if it is featuring Zandra Rhodes merchandise.

So there's your situation – a mannequin in a messy bed lounging around dolling herself up – complete with a night stand and an alarm clock. She also has her beauty supplies at hand: a brush, nail polish and even some sort of soothing night mask.

The bed, in retrospect, was literally a mess. I think we just had a box and put some sheets on it. The comforter was store merchandise as Bonwit's also had a small Home Collection. The rattan screen was not my style, so it was probably just sitting around somewhere in storage.

The mannequin – the sole Rootstein in the store - does show off both herself and the gown to great effect. But, wait – what are those things on her feet? Shoes? Not even slippers – but real shoes? This, on a mannequin in lingerie, when we usually eschewed shoes on most mannequins most of the time in all kinds of merchandise? Who knows why? And, yes, this is the window that was most times dedicated to men's fashion.

In the end, not one of my best window displays – but hey, they can't all be winners. Sometimes we just needed a quickie window display to fill in some dead time in the calendar. I wanted to include this as it's a good shot of the Rootstein mannequin.

Plate 20

Plates 21, 22….The Party

In the 1970's there was a style of window display called "situation windows" – meaning the design was of a real or lifelike setting. New York stores in particular were involved in this style of display window design. Henri Bendel had many – Bloomingdales, even Saks – and others - think mannequins with shopping carts, like they were in a grocery store, or queuing up behind a stanchion rope as if they were in line at a bank.

This style was not exactly new – stores had off and on being doing it for decades – it was just another way of designing a display window – but in the 70's they just became a little more outrageous at times. I was not a huge fan of this style, especially if the execution was sloppy - I even had done my own versions at times.

In mid-summer 1978, I wanted to do a little more of an elaborate window than I had been attempting at Bonwit's thus far. I thought maybe it would attract more attention as it wouldn't be my usual minimalistic style. It would also utilize the full width of the display window.

My assistant and I decided on a party theme. We could utilize some of the new Nissen mannequins I had just purchased and mix them with the DG Williams girls plus the one Rootstein. (I was never, also, a huge fan of mixing mannequin companies in the same window, and I had let this go early on at Bonwit's due to the scarcity of mannequins in general. Also – since this was a party theme we thought that different makers of mannequins would go along with the theme). The store had plenty of antiques to create a lifelike "room" plus a few recent prop purchases could make it appear even more like a room in a home.

I'm not sure if I bought these extra props exclusively for this window design – I think I did. The silkscreened cloud panel, balustrade and louvered window screens (both made of Styrofoam) – were all from Niedermaier. The decision also was made to remove the white floor pads to expose the parquet wood floor – to further heighten the effect of a residence.

As I've mentioned before, the door to the window was directly behind the cash wrap of the hosiery department. The sales ladies were used to us bringing next to nothing in prop-wise, so we weren't much of a nuisance usually. Then, we're hauling in sofas and chairs all of a sudden – geez, to listen to them kvetch you would have thought we were driving a Buick in or something.

This window was also planned as a two part window – my first – and last I believe. Part two – Plate 22– "After The Party".

As I recall – everyone thought the windows were a success, but I soon went back to the minimalism that was more my style.

Plate 21

Plate 22

Plate 23….A Men's Athletic Window

Today a lot of people, men and women – but especially men, spend most of their off work hours dressed in generic, or item specific athletic apparel. This was not so much the case in 1978. This window shows two men's mannequins – one, in what looks to be tennis gear, and the other one in some sort of street wear athletic apparel. It looks like it might have been velour – complete with cargo pant pockets.

By now, even the casual reader will have noticed the three dimensional white lettering on the bottom of the window mullion surround. I had purchased similar white lettering at my previous display department positions. It seems dated now – like much in this book – but at the time it helped "tell the story" as well as where the merchandise was located and designers' names etc.

This is also one of the pictures that I took in 35 MM slide format. All of these pictures were faint and suffer from the reflections from outside. But this simple window typifies the style that I was most comfortable with – a clean, crisp white box and bringing in just enough propping to tell a story.

Plate 24.....Cultural Institution Windows

Department and Specialty Stores in any city were often requested in those days by cultural institutions to include their posters from their most current exhibitions in a display window.

This – the usually "Men's Window"- was a window for the Chicago Field Museum of Natural History. This was roughly late spring or early summer when I had purchased this new Nissen mannequin. This is also one of the pictures I took in 35 MM slide format.

Even though this was not for the King Tut exhibition that was traveling the country during the 70's – that had been in Chicago the prior year – it was right at the height of popularity for Steve Martin's song, and Saturday Night Live performance of, "King Tut". My assistant and I both loved Steve Martin and the song and we had a lot of laughs imitating Mr. Martin complete with all of the hand gestures (YouTube it): "King Tut - Born in Arizona, got a condo made of stone ah". It was a 1978 thing.

GOLDEN TREASURES
FIELD MUSEUM
FEBRUARY
OF GOLD   JEWE

Plate 25....A Summer Window

These beautiful silk chiffon gowns from the Designer Salon were incredible – several with gorgeous diaphanous sleeves. Perfect for the "arms up" gals! For once these mannequins wouldn't need to be "holding something up" – they were showing off the gowns' designs.

Having operational fans in a display window was nothing new at the time. I had remembered a photo of a B. Altman window in New York from a subscription photography service at the time out of New York called "Views and Reviews" published by Retail Reporting Corporation New York. They sent out a monthly packet of very high quality 8" x 10" photos of New York display windows. There was also a brief narrative on each pic of what that editor thought might be the design intent. They were a great source of inspiration. Depending on what store I worked at the time we always had them plus older pics as well – some going back to the early 1960's.

The B Altman fan window – four running antique fans on pedestals of different heights and two mannequins in identical poses in a "blacked out" window – blacked out – meaning the floor and walls were all either painted black or had been covered in black felt. The photo, also featured in the 1978 book, The American Store Window", by Leonard S. Marcus, is from 1974, a transition year for store windows themselves. A lot of Display Directors at that time were going from a completely blacked out window to an all-white window. The blacked out windows had been the norm for many years – I'm not sure how long, but they had been since I first started out in the business. One of the first things I did when I started at Bonwit's was to paint all of the windows white from black – and make white vinyl floor pads.

So, there is nothing new in my window here, although I wanted to update the idea. I rummaged around the storage places in the store and found five pedestals and painted them white. I bought the oscillating fans – all the same – at Ace Hardware and positioned them front and center. I decided to ignore the cords. As we more than not did, we left the mannequins barefoot, with one mannequin holding her shoes and another apparently having kicked them off to better catch the breeze. I'm pretty sure the beautiful gown with the printed scene was designed by Hanae Mori, the Japanese designer, who is still alive as of this writing. As I recall now the window was well received by just about everyone!

Plate 25

Plate 26….The Missoni Shop – Dealing With the Building Cross Beams

Missoni moved permanently into the northwest corner of the Bonwit Teller store in the spring/summer of 1978. This is also the northwest corner of the John Hancock building where the shop would be fronted on two sides with plate glass – open to the outside. As noted before, the cross beams - structural as well as design elements – were a pesky annoyance at times. One of these beams begins its angular ascent in the northwest corner of the building where the Missoni Shop-In-Shop would be.

We had already given Missoni the main fashion window for a two week run with the oversized "hang tags". I was trying to come up with an idea for the opening of the shop itself. I wanted to somehow use the crossbeams as part of the window design. I could use the hang tags of course – but how? I had by this time purchased a few new mannequins. One of these new girls was a seated Nissen.

The crossbeam is in the entire frame of this window. It begins its ascent in the south, front part of this shop. The crossbeam actually starts out flat – coming out of the south wall of the shop a few feet before it starts to angle. This would be a perfect place to put a seated mannequin holding one of the Missoni hang tags. Although she can't be seen that well in this photo, I put one of the DG Williams mannequins – the leaning gal against a wall (see Plate 26, far right) – lying flat on her back so it appears she has her left foot against the wall and her right foot on the beam. I had used her in this floor position before (see Plate 6) and it seemed to work at the time – the reader will have to decide on their own whether or not it did here too.

This was my first attempt to bring in the crossbeam as part of the story – embrace it if you will – rather than trying to obscure it or mask it off. (as the North Face currently is doing as of this writing). So to round out the rest of the window that was open to the store, I placed two other new Nissen mannequins on what looks like a coffee table with their requisite hang tags and with a tag on the beam as well. We had gotten special new lettering to go with the Missoni logo – "At Bonwit Teller" – to go on the crossbeam. Whether all of this stayed this way after the shop opened– I doubt it – I just don't remember.

Plate 26

Plate 27….Crossbeam – An Intimate Apparel Window

This display window did not exist, I don't believe, until I was at Bonwit's. I could be wrong – but it's been so long ago, I really don't remember.

Possible scenarios:

-The window plate glass had been "blacked out" with reverse paint from the interior. I had maintenance scrape the paint off and paint the window walls and beam white (I may have painted it white – but I am sure I would not have taken the black paint off of the plate glass).

-The interior of the window – the beam, walls etc. had been "blacked out" so as to disappear and I had them painted white (or I did).

In either scenario, it's somewhat obvious that the space had been originally intended as some sort of display window, even with the beam in it – note to the far right what appears to be a door – and to the far left – a wall that ends the opening of the window, though the beam keeps ascending.

In any event, and with my speculation as to the origins of the window, I decided to give it a try.

The Drury Lane theater (or, as I liked to call it at the time, the "Dreary" Lane) was directly across from Bonwit Teller on Chestnut St. in Water Tower Place. Water Tower Place had been completed in late 1975 and besides containing an eight floor vertical shopping mall, apartments and a Ritz Carleton hotel – it also had a legit theater. The theater asked us to include a promotional poster for this show "I Love My Wife".

All I can remember is this image – we seemed to do a lot of lingerie – or Intimate Apparel (as my very own lettering indicates) display windows. Again, the comforter and pillows were store merchandise, the gown is fabulous, the Rootstein mannequin is glamourous, the radiators look great climbing up into infinity on the crossbeam – and the gal has kicked off her shoes, of course (as well as, apparently, "drying off" a few "intimates" on one of the radiators) – but ultimately, does the window work? In hindsight, I would say, no.

I don't recall that we used the window again. This photo is actually dated on the back, 10-30-78, so I'm thinking we probably didn't, at least as long as I was there. But, at least I had attempted several times to confront these beams in a creative manner rather than obscuring them or masking them off from view.

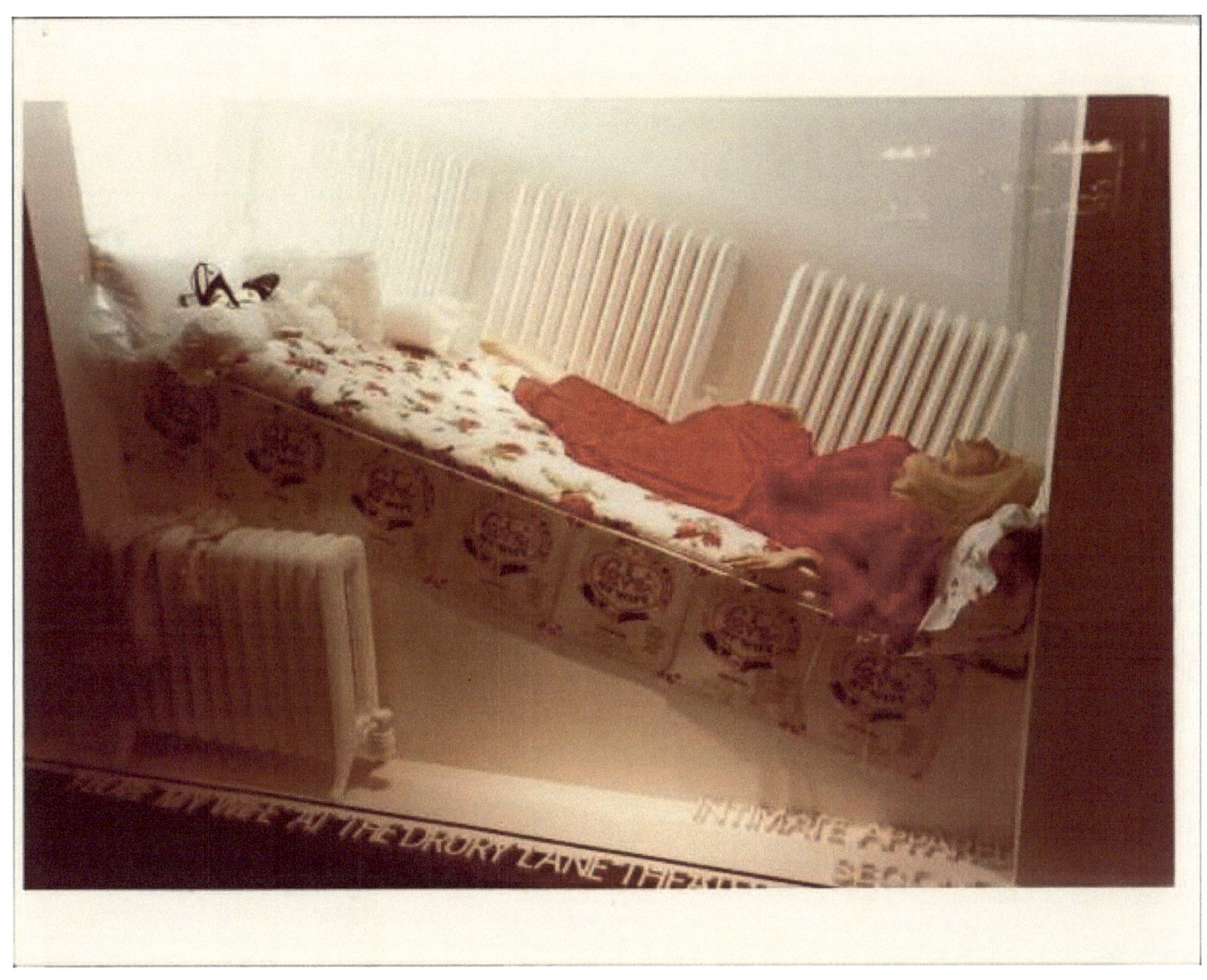

Plate 27

Plate 28....The Veiled Reds

This display window was either late summer or early fall. It was essentially a cosmetics launch for "Ultima II – The Veiled Reds", but of course showcased these fabulous designer duds as well. The name of the designer escapes me now. The designer department did carry a lot of Georgio St. Angelo and Valentino – amongst many – but who knows?

Another clue might have been my window copy, but, unfortunately, I cropped this photo for a portfolio entry many years ago.

As I had done occasionally, I positioned the mannequins and the props in the center of the display window and ignored both ends of the window. I had just purchased these classic, Grecian head busts and columns from Niedermaier. All of a sudden I'm leaving minimalism for the classics? Hardly. I was just creating a "marriage" of sorts of these two styles. A classic form within a minimal setting.

But I still felt it needed a little drama added to the mix. Veiled. Veils. Netting was always a nice, inexpensive prop. I draped the DG Williams mannequins in black netting and added the more expensive tulle over the busts and columns. I dialed down the lighting for even more drama. The result is one of my favorite windows of the entire year.

Plate 28

Plate 29….Another Lingerie Window

What, another lingerie window? Apparently sales must have been good in the Intimate Apparel Department. This window picture is dated 9-24-78.

This type of glittery, shimmering, silk like strands hanging from the ceiling grid are common today as a prop, and variations on them, but at the time they were kind of a new item. It was well into the time that I had added the chair rail to the walls. I've spread the mannequins out into the window more – today I would want five rather than four mannequins. Or maybe I was counting the prop as the fifth element? I'm really not quite sure when I started using the "odd number" system of elements in a display.

By this point doing something with the shoes other than wearing them (or not - as in the cross beam window – (Plate 27) was a hallmark of our lingerie windows (and others too). Here, the only mannequins I can detect holding a pair of shoes are the gals at each end. Maybe the mannequin second from the left has kicked hers off at her feet – there appears to be something there – I certainly don't remember, that's for sure. Also, if you look closely, the mannequin on the far left is holding one of these silky strands as it hits the floor.

Plate 29

Plate 30….Some New Mannequins

The Nissen mannequins pictured here were not as interesting or as dramatic as the DG Williams mannequins but, we needed some Junior mannequins. Here are a few of these mannequins (although the two on the left are Missy – not Juniors).Nissen's were popular at the time, and as I recall – they were a bit less expensive than Rootsteins and had a quicker turnaround time.

The chairs pictured here were from the stores furniture collection. While not antiques at the time, they were form an earlier era even though they look very modern. The chair was designed by Marcel Bruer in 1925 and is in production to this day. It was nicknamed the Wassily for the artist Kandinsky because of his admiration for the chair. It's hard to say when these chairs were produced but since the store was opened concurrent with the Hancock building being completed in 1969 they were probably form that time period. Obviously there were a lot of these Wassily chairs sitting around the store at my disposal – I didn't buy them, I know that. Because I was only utilizing the center portion of the window for the mannequins, I can't tell how many of the chairs were actually in the window as the two end ones are cropped off in this photo. I'm hoping there was an odd number.

Also – I was never one to want to put a hat on every single mannequin, so I'm not sure about that one. But, the overall effect of the chair repetition I like very much.

Plate 30

Plates 31, 32….Safari Shop - A Seasonal Transition Window

One of my "go to" prop resources for many years actually began in 1978. The hardware store. What a great place to browse around for, not only props – but ideas as well.

We had a window coming due from the Safari Shop for a fall "transition" set of clothing from the Dutch designer Koos Van Den Akker. I don't recall why it was called the Safari Shop other than it was designer sportswear. Transition in retail fashion speak means what it says – while it's still summer, we're not going to scare you with all the new bulky, heavy fall sweaters and coats – but – we'll "transition" you psychologically with more autumn like colors and slightly heavier fabrications to get you in the mood to at least think about buying fall clothes.

These Van Den Akker designs were funky for the time – quilted, bib like, – patch worky – kind of – electric. So, I'm in Ace Hardware looking around and I see these gray metal boxes with a red handles on them – I wasn't quite sure what they were – something to do with an electrical thing I figured – and all these brightly colored plastic coated wires – and I thought – here's my prop.

Of course the way I set these props up made no sense electrically – but I lined 'em up on the wall anyway with the wires coming out of them helter skelter – and – voila – window display design on a dime - cheap and cheerful as they say.

Plate 31

Close up of A Seasonal Transition
Window

Plate 32

Plate 33….A Halloween Window

In 1978 Halloween had not quite yet become the event it is today – but still something to work with – a concept. I had purchased these sort of - Harlequin meets Mime – masks, if not for the purpose of a Halloween window, they certainly worked out well for a generic sort of Halloween. Although it's hard to tell – and even harder for me to remember – they were made of porcelain I believe with multi-color ribbons cascading down the sides.

You can see the end of the window copy "… Black Magic". I believe the entire copy read "That Old Black Magic" Original, huh?

Now that I have looked more closely at these pictures in the last few weeks than I have in decades, I am struck by how some of these gowns are so revealing. Notice on the mannequin to the far right, the deep plunging halter style décolletage – a very Halston 70's style look. It might even have been a Halston.

Note also the mink coat that the mannequin on the far left is holding. Furs are not as popular as they used to be. The Fur Salon at Bonwit Teller was actually a concession – or – a leased department – most fur departments were in those days. It was just too costly to invest in fur inventory. It also required specialized training on the various types of animal pelts used as well as special air cooled vaults in which to store them. The Fur Salon at Bonwit's was leased by Maximilian of New York. I remember a charity event they hosted that year that the movie star Rita Hayworth co-chaired - we were able to peek into the salon to get a glimpse of her.

Again, in retrospect, I'm not too thrilled with all of the hats – but – it was Halloween.

Plate 33

Plate 34....I Promise it's the Last Lingerie Window!

As 1978 was coming to an end – and, also, my end of working at Bonwit Teller – I did these last few holiday windows.

There would have been a series of holiday windows in the main fashion window. This is the only picture, unfortunately, that I have from that time.

I had decided to install a glossy red vinyl floor in the Delaware window for the duration of the year. This photo is dated 11-28-78, so it was probably one of the first of the series of windows. I believe this would also be the first time I simply strung miniature Christmas lights from the ceiling grid to the floor and called it a proper window display. To me, having the red floor already said Christmas – add some miniature lights and that was enough as far as I was – and still am – concerned. I still wander how I got away with such simple window displays.

I also always loved how the red floor and lights reflect on the rain soaked pavement visible here in front of the window.

Plate 34

Plate 35….A Men's Holiday Window

As 1978 continued to run out – here we are with my last men's window for 1978. A very simple winter scene with the dude decked out and dashing in formal attire – complete with a "snowbrella". But not just any mannequin - check this guy out with the mustache. I must have purchased him at some point during the year, as the only other men's mannequins I remember at Bonwit's were the semi-abstract, glossy, white painted guys.

If you look carefully in the back – the door is partially open. My guess is – because it probably happened in the past – that one of the Men's Department sales staff had either sold something off of the mannequin – a scarf maybe - and had replaced it but hadn't closed the door all the way. I was never present when the photographer took the shots so I didn't have time to edit the window.

Plate 35

Plate 36….My Last Designer Holiday Window

Actually, I don't remember if this was my last window display at all – Holiday or otherwise. I just wanted to end the book with it because it's dramatic.

It's also – if you've been paying attention at all – what I've described as usually the Men's window. I think I can safely say, at this point, that really wasn't so.

The evening gown with a matching cape was gorgeous and, I think, timeless. I'd like to think it was Valentino or Dior – but I really don't remember and I am not that much of a fashion history buff to know immediately from one look without researching it a bit. The asymmetrical necklace is also timeless and with an interesting form having no clasp.

The DG Williams mannequin pose was my favorite of the whole bunch – this leaning against a wall pose (or lying down on the floor) was always a dramatic pose that could show off a gown in a very dramatic manner. This gown was no different. The hair style was stylish at the time – now, not so much. The lone prop – the antique chair – not my favorite style of prop – but perfect for this scene – holding her evening bag.

In retrospect there are two things that bother me about this display window now. The first is what appears to be a fabric tie for the cape that's not been tucked away properly out of view. My guess is that we wanted to show the gown completely and if we had tied the cape with the tie – it would have obscured the gown too much. Number two is the fact that the gown is somewhat transparent and the mannequin's torso seam – where she separates from her bottom half - is held together with tape that shows through the gown! Fashion mannequins such as these were fragile in many ways. In transporting them to the display window and in the process of striking them to the floor, the torso would sometimes twist and want to separate from her legs. We would frequently tape that seam to prevent that from happening. Again, with me not being there in the evening with the photographer, these small but important details slip by. But it's still a good shot to end the book with!

Plate 36

Background on the Building and the Store

The non-traditional style of the Hancock building - set back with a sunken plaza in front of it, - created a non-traditional arrangement of the display windows. Traditional department and specialty stores had their main "fashion" windows right in front adjacent to sidewalks. This was a form of advertising and marketing that had been in place since the beginning of department stores – think Macy's or Chicago's own Marshall Field's.

Also, being located in an architecturally important building that in and of itself was an instant landmark upon its completion in 1969, was an unusual location for a specialty store. The store front facing Michigan Avenue itself did not have the store's main fashion window. That was located on the north side of the store on Delaware adjacent to the entrance to the residences of the Hancock building. Maybe this was done to entice the well-to-do residents to more easily view the exclusive fashions? The design of the building? I don't know.

All I know is it was frustrating to have the main fashion window located at the side of the building. It was also a very large window measuring 30 feet wide with a more traditional depth of around 6 or 7 feet. There was also an extremely wide expanse of sidewalk in front of the window – indeed, around the entire building. All undoubtedly part of the architects' overall design of the buildings' "set back" from the street. As my career continued in later years, I would encounter many situations with the architectural design of a stores' display window that was less than satisfactory for a window display designer to actually use in an effective way. Never let an architect totally design a display window. At the very least get a window designer involved in the design process.

The store front itself – which currently houses two stores, The North Face and Best Buy – not exactly chic fashion destinations – had two entrances with revolving doors with very low key, uninteresting block letter signs on the building front. Both front entrances were flanked by "open" display windows. The back of each window was a traditional paned glass window.

The south, front corner of the building – where Best Buy currently is - was where Hermes had their leased Shop-In-Shop. They too had an entrance display window that I was contractually obligated to change once a month or each season. It was always the same set up – with the saddle and everything – just different merchandise. They also had shadow box style windows where their beautiful scarves were simply stretched flat over boards. There were also two other shadow box style windows on the north side of the building that featured jewelry and accessories.

As I look at the building today, It's hard to place the entrance doors. It seems to me that the south entrance has been altered – but I really can't remember. What I can say is that the building isn't nearly as elegant without the Bonwit Teller store.